DEEP SINGH

Immature LINES

From Raw Emotions to Refined Rhymes

Exploring the Heart's Landscape

BlueRose ONE.com
Stories Matter
NewDelhi • London

BLUEROSE PUBLISHERS
India | U.K.

BlueRoseONE.com
Stories Matter
NewDelhi • London

For permissions requests or inquiries regarding this publication, please contact:

BLUEROSE PUBLISHERS
www.BlueRoseONE.com
info@bluerosepublishers.com
+91 8882 898 898
+4407342408967

ISBN: 978-93-5819-883-6

Cover Design: Muskan Sachdeva
Typesetting: Pooja Sharma

First Edition: February 2024

Editor's Note

The presented collection of poems demonstrates a versatile and expressive writing style, blending various themes and subjects with an intricate use of language. The poet showcases a deep engagement with both natural and human elements, portraying a keen observation of life's nuances. The poems are marked by a rich descriptive quality that vividly paints images of landscapes, characters, and emotions.

The poet employs a diverse range of themes, ranging from introspective musings on life and existence to societal commentary and observations on human behavior. This versatility allows for a dynamic reading experience, offering readers a tapestry of emotions and ideas. The thematic exploration extends from the personal to the universal, capturing the essence of the human experience across different contexts.

One noticeable aspect of the writing style is the effective use of vivid and evocative imagery. Descriptions such as "In dense, greenwoods where pines grow" or "A rhythmic galloping and rhythmic clattering" transport the reader into the scenes being depicted. This skillful use of imagery not only adds aesthetic value but also serves as a powerful tool to convey the poet's thoughts and emotions.

The narrative flow of the poems is often nonlinear, inviting readers to navigate through the verses with an element of surprise. This nonlinear structure contributes to the complexity of the work, keeping the audience engaged and prompting them to explore the deeper layers of meaning embedded within the verses. The use of enjambment and varied stanza lengths further enhances the rhythmic flow and adds a dynamic quality to the poetry.

The poet also demonstrates a penchant for exploring philosophical and existential themes, delving into questions of life, death, morality, and the human condition. This introspective approach adds depth to the collection, inviting readers to reflect on their own experiences and perspectives. The contemplative tone is accentuated by the incorporation of rhetorical questions, inviting readers into a dialogue with the poet's thoughts.

The collection showcases a mastery of language, with a nuanced play of words and expressions. The poet employs rhyme and rhythm judiciously, creating a musicality that enhances the aesthetic appeal of the verses. The choice of words, whether in describing the beauty of nature or the complexities of human relationships, reflects a careful consideration of language's power to evoke emotions and convey meaning.

While the themes explored are often profound and thought-provoking, there is also a touch of simplicity and accessibility in the language used. This allows a wide range of readers to connect with the verses, irrespective of their familiarity with poetic conventions. The blend of sophistication and accessibility contributes to the inclusivity of the collection.

In conclusion, the writing style exhibited in this collection is characterized by its versatility, vivid imagery, philosophical depth, and a mastery of language. The poet skillfully navigates through a diverse array of themes, providing readers with a multifaceted and engaging literary experience. The poems leave a lasting impression by resonating with the universal aspects of the human experience and inviting readers to contemplate the intricacies of life.

Contents

01. Owner of Woods

All alone, in the desolate plane
Who seizes reign and who holds the chain?
Who sent them all into the woods?
Either are thirsty or in search of food
Begins gathering what they can
Enjoin chirp, breeze around
When cuckoo in delight flutter wings
Pines whirl and creepers cling
Tender bud to mature bloom
In short duration you touch the sky
How do you run, how dare you fly?
You grow up and relations tether
Mother Father to Sister Brothers
Wood for you turn into world
Forget thy entrance overlooked your roll
Who tests thy flight and what keeps thee on track?
You keep on going what retrieve thee back
Have you ever realised? Who set that trap?
Begins plagiarism, like dense horde
In negligence how, you trod

How thorns were trampled in way you met
How fervently the cologne you kept
Smugness arise with thy selection
Loathing begins with thy aversion
Thy Extol swell thy acquaintance
How it reacts when words are astringent
How it seems that world is MINE
Let me trod where SUN does shine
In every nook you explore
Sense of amassing make you roll
Oh! Glutton you hoard a mound
Eye Invisible watch this alone
He makes you secure when you fly
Remove obstacles when you walk
Compute flaws in your talk
With your breath It stray in your soul
Despite of eyes, linger in dark
Is it possible to take it out whole?
What you hoard on in a little rest
There is the MASTER who holds the chain
Who had a rein and rode the Woods
How can you hinder His Laws?
He is the Master and puppet we are

02. Clinic

Was it necessary to pay such a visit?
Pale, pooped and sick face
A mate ailing bit
Howling in pain but smoke to inhale
Gate opened and crowd in
Folks hustle to the first turn,
Fee three scores pocket win,
Consoling starts to turn by turn.
Mixed creeds and tribes assemble,
Rainbow it seems, seven in one.
United they were with no favouritism
Father of Nation has not foreseen
The Story begin, till date it reign
When it appears aristocrats first,
We the Common, gazing down
Turn for fourteen reverse forty-first
Waiting, watching the inequity grown
A fat clamber the porch,
Obesity in body and laziness attack,
Consultant advised to not take much,

Took prescription, not thanking back,
Brood for long indoor cavern,
Hang about when ridiculous elucidate
Adult approaches with eyes to heaven
Declare boorishly, wild should tolerate
Oh! These words triggered my heart
Dressed poorly with heel cracks
Little sweet buds just to graft
Tread miles through hill tracks.
But these urban meters away
Just on two tyres, but wish first,
He deliberately forgot to convey,
The Message of well-being, creating mistrust.
Hour repose when he faces the doctor
See, pills paper and pieces of advice, again,
Thrice a day a bit meal after,
For a month repeat the same.
We both returned with a flushing face.
Murmuring about this long race........

03. She Was Black

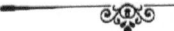

She was moulded in the south of my nation
Was little dark but temperate
Fighting for livelihood in north of my nation
Her dark future and rebuke in fate.
Shady complexion with stately height,
Cloud moon-like gleaming but alert,
Face round, curled upright
Calm, voice and sympathetic heart
Oh! God her destitute future
Working in the shower, without oilskin
Abdomen wants with sixteenth creature
Engaged in the sand, cutting iron-tin
Latest born should have dwelled in love
Should lose herself in fair face
Chant their tale in delicious move
And his beauty, she should trace
Labourers' hands, boorish with sand,
Shall have a pencil and tutor's face.
Accompanied by the chorus with patriotic band
Or a prayer in the shrine on her anniversary

What I feign, would it breed the same?
I want her gleaming but God knows
These lines, whenever one will browse
So, a twinkling one shall ever glow.

04. A Boring Period

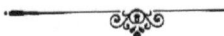

In two hours, repose
The noise arouse,
Impose on us twice a week.
Let me keep my pouch of divine
Sipping of which is a benediction of mind
Uncouth, scowl endorse to wine
Refrain from it what`s mine
Owner knows, what hens and cocks are,
Quarrel, laceration or slur, it's to them.
What's to me, ruined your future
I would not reap this invalid sow
Why befool me oh! You cheater
Ripe or raw left them to owe
They have a boat and let them row
If the goal is there, let them go
Wait and watch till the end of the show....

05. Her Immortal Life

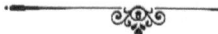

She was born where the sun rarely glows
In dense, greenwoods where pines grow,
Crying, dazing in Mom's arm,
Spontaneous blessing of beauty and charm
Father's affection, eye star of mother,
Darling bud of gleaming summer,
Her beauty can't be faded in the noon,
Comparison in complexion better than the moon,
Low musical, but calm one,
Akin nightingale in her tune
She was dwarf but moulded in skills,
Like a psyche, a queen of hills,
In maiden world seeming one
And in Bud's garden contrast none
Boss in sylphs beyond description
Dawning fragrance and lilac coloration
Divine of her eyes inspired a youth
Who stakes his heart and his soul?
Dreams of romance for a virtuous lady.
In her love, he got Crazy

Grassy plush in pluvial forest
Arms embraced where love grows't
Surplus kissing, in moaning voice
Historic couple seemed to rejoice.
Their promises, oath of lifespan
Was firm, thinks every man.
Adorned by others she refrained
When she said I have done
Choice is immortal, youth is one.
Oracle says it's mine,
When they celebrate the seventh Valentine,
Superstitious prediction of eight, believe none
Sweet or tragic, God knows one.
When the sun had set and evening began,
At a fixed time, the death bargain
Opponents of her love triggered down.
Oh no one there all alone
Sleep forever in loud sound
Tangled in air, all around
Why it happened is still a mystery
Now for me it is a page of history

06. Dawn at Bus Stop

Slumber ends and the dawn broke
Rooster swank, cabs crawl,
Oh! Bus stop appears awake
Hum, puffing and calls.
Passengers have set their goals.
Engine blast and tyres roll.
Cups, plates, tea man enjoin.
In a metrical voice, he used to call
Less milk and water all.
Morn spending open heart
Hawkers and fruit sellers
Melodious tune try to persuade.
Under tree fortune tellers
Swindle customer akin to horse and rider
Courteous statements squeeze their pockets
Go ahead whatever they ate,
They have heads and we have scissors
Quantity cost less, double its rate.
What a fine you got around
Cool breeze and wet season,

It is difficult to stay in the chilling cold.

Travel there, no reason

If I'll be asked hey! Why you?

Just answer, it`s there

To chat and for humour,

Share with us o! Dear.

07. Mother Father

Mother and Father in the world to me
The pair of diamonds that always gleam
Mother`s eyes have profuse love
Presence of Father makes me glow
Nobody in the world love us true
As much as our adoring parents do
Our gladness is their charm
Shine on our faces bring them charm
They are God's most precious gift
Thank God for that valuable gift

08. Bitter Drink

Sour in taste, like humiliation
But for honesty it's treatment
One who devote to evil, contagion
Reality, truth has final consignment
No one drinks until the disease is fatal
A pick pocket or bit carouse
Hate in your own use to hurtle
Perch or drabble in voice arouse
Credulous one, cobweb by tickle
Or fair or chum`s invalid company
Bribe or corruption always ripple
In dark world indulged so many.
Have thee ever had "The bitter drink"
Swallowed once, need no more
No need to accustom, but credulous shrinks
Swallowed once, need no more
Treated once, always remain
But required more if fatal disease
Hounds one, they need again
Remedy of which finds another ease.

09. Homeland

Dense are pines in my Eden,
The past annals of several goddesses
Oh! Serenity and is fear-ridden
Beads of garland, no discrimination,
Dawn begin with the chirping of cuckoo
How sweet are songs of summer?
Sun stream upon hills and herb
Later a day began warmer and warmer.
Women after prayer, a rim with butter
Earthen pots and water so cool................
A rhythmic tune of flute, young utter
Swimming kids, holly pools.
Goose murmured and went out farmer
With a pair of oxen and begin ploughing,
Joining hands his women too
Milk and butter kids enjoying
Chilling huts in warmer season
Buds, flowers, bloomy-bloomy
Picturesque sight oh! No reason
Blabbing on cots in mooney-mooney

Psalm together, by tracking miles,
No contamination, if rich or poor
Remote are houses, but love dwell,
Hospitality keen, peep any door.
Cattle, sheep, taken out for grazing
There in, a couple singing
Rejoicing The nature with little drizzling
Eclogue of love, the flute playing
Self-dependent, no urban air
Winter approaches with snowflake
White coins, roving clear
How to come out oh! My dear
Spend some months and emerge again
Give off cocoons and sowing grains
So beautiful is my homeland.

10. If I Were God

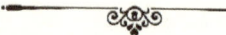

Of new kind will be this creation
Quite different with variety variation,
Of my desires and devotion.
An echo of love and great furtherance
No conception, without gestation
Like seeds in plants and hanging fruits
Transmute into kids in proper limitation
Agony free, happy and smart
Overall a painless process
Get rid of this pawky zoo
Volunteer conversation and food wants
In symbiotic act, affection too
No hatred no contamination
Brotherhood among each other
No terrorism and no degradation
Ecstasy, no moan, brutality no further
Reverence to souls no arrogance
Every organism, Honour each other
Truth sways, hate no neither
Only, Cardiac link of people with me
No fear of mine, no salute to me.

11. Gate

It was architecture in redoubt
Guarded by red coats and now judicial
Surrounded with belle, young and adult
Tables, chairs, knavish and quizzical
I entered just to hang about
Stand aside at the noisy pavement
Gazing eagerly, as people move
Heating noon, hazy hazy
Curiosity increase and sit down
Tired repose, dazy dazy.
Lawyers as liars and assistants as goons
Little work and handful of dollars
Where is harmony as aristocrat frisky-frisky
Poor like me roll over collars
Who will dare to expose this legislation?
As common entrance and diverse dealing
Pretending of slumber in open eyes

12. Silence

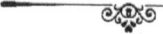

It's a weapon of non-violence
God forbid! But is silence
Fob, cheater no matter
If cozen, judged no need to utter
Reason in the silence of mine
How to keep silent when it`s true
How to remain silent
When it needs to prove
If by design one raised your anger
Calmly ask a reason man
Only react when feeling in danger
Roused you, lean with silence
Let's chat no place for violence.
Entangled in critics listen by heart
Be positive and think of fault
Correction by self is self-mastery.
No room to blame, so do it greatly.

***

13. As Soldier

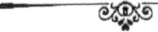

I need to go and shake my hand
Eccentricity, but know anthropology
Later a reveille, with morn band
Chastisement, if mistake but apology
Oozing sack, but have to run.
If sluggishness proved then extra run
All forgotten in batch fun
Have to toil in mountain and plains
In combat, a cutlass in hand
Sack dorsal, with a gun to move
Or with binnacle, inspecting around
Opponent`s mutilation, show the white feather,
Do or die it's patriotic urge
Enervate them or entangle either
Triumphant celebration with harping emerge
Or taste a divine and cremation
Barren hills or in woods
It's often called drink for the nation
Soul is immortal and bodies are fragile
It has to wane now and then

And will awarded for task of mine
Home will wait sun to shine
A fair page with congratulation,
Or will moan, on fate of mine
Obituary in daily news in the nation.

14. Horse Cart and Rider

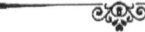

Harnessed firmly, with nasal strap
Ferric toes hammered nail
It's cob duty, from its natal
Lassoed and restrained, opposing fail
A wooden chaise, clenched firmly
Built stylishly with different dimensions
Shady and soft the roof creation
With a black beard and curled whisker
Tinted turban, golden brown
Whip in hand intellectually wiser
Sincere but jocose born
A rhythmic galloping
And rhythmic clattering
Here goes the wheel rumbling
How does a whip hoop in the air?
O what an echo of unity and art.
He loves cob as well as cart
Where is the whole world?
Where is the man?
What's bad if will breed the same
In nations all over the world
To owe their sweat no false fame

15. A Mason

He's Argus! Have you ever seen?
Keep reflecting even in a dream
And is wet in hot and cold
Raw; How easily does he mould?
Moving trowel in rhythmic motion
Adjusting bricks and silicates
Firm bonding and wall formation
Petite to gigantic he insulates
Attempt is to make them firm
Pillared it in systematic roof
Historic structure in air swims
And floor, almost in the rood
Who is needed to develop the Nation?
Architecture of the Nation is when
Foe and fan always keep,
Individuals shall keep unity among them
Sorrows and joy together shall reap
Once stabilized shall never collapse
Huge if constructed can match Alps
Foundation of Pillars is if the strong
Then hostile attempts will never prolong.

16. Call On

What when you don't know
A call on a crooked head
To defeat you will bow
Nodding tearing and face red
Oh! Oh! Its ring
Your fans chaffy call
Gal like makeup
If asleep you will crawl
Tickle you and your wife
With kids what's papa
Rare answer and will flee
Glove in head oh! No Papa
Fair reception and to have rest
Other with Negus and wine
Hum eggs you and next
Dabbled in sipping will enjoin
When it knells with an appalling sound
Spirit desolate and body to hate
Immoveable lying on ground
People mourn, oh! Oh! Fate

Shrouded in red or in white
Eyes suffused and go on
In sandalwood or soil is right.
Death bargain at last call on.

17. Rainy Days

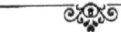

Days are rainy in our fate
Liable one we intend to hate
If impeded on have to tolerate
Stain in fortune cards may have taken
Posterity ruined. We are destitute
Wind is rough, so acute
Our own blood dabble in creating
What's mom milk turn cruel treating
Behave like sheep tigers around
Where is the sky and where are ground?
Life and death seem on palm
How to utter truth so remain calm
Day passes easily chatting with friends
Pseudo alive and all hope ends
In play with kids or routine work
Night begins with window knock or door jerk
We are accustomed of weekly sounds
Produced from either side all around
A rhythmic work in this way
And all of us think of rainy days

What's with us on only half of it?
Endure this apathy think a bit
Of those who lose or migrate
Asked when eye tears narrate
Oh! It was self-God's creation
Of marvellous sight and old tradition
Where in soothing and bloomy blossom
Of equal rank and no egoism
In a vale where we lived
Was calm and agony relieved
Everything charming and so cute
Increases beauty by rippling mute
In summer we burst out of cocoon
From winter snowy puffing woollen
And the coin storm of snowflake
This covers the dell and pretty lake
Our salutary vale we leave,
Mosque voice in morn dawn grew
In temple and shrine a prayer murmur
Morning or evening winter or summer
Being bit confliction the enemy succeed
Hostility between two so breed
Vocal-bribe and tickle them
Weapons, bombs man to men

These all terminate a long chain
Of schism and bloody rain
Wild treated and remorseless
Human worthy blood seem worthless
A morning chirping turn in reveille
A clattering rhyme of scouts prevail
Life lost in gun sound
Tangle in every nook all around
To face drastic rapine
Rebels impose bloody brine
Women loss and were relicted
Some pseudo alive and were stilted
Huts in fire even tombs too
Everyday encounter in human's zoo
Among them we are escape goats
Smother us but liable to wait
Every day dawn with demise cry
Mother wives in arid eyes
Son daughter or for husband
Like maize harvesting end
Where is humanity where is right
Contradiction in home let them fight
Its minute world is wide
Formal consoling and put aside

If life will be then can germinate
That's why we migrate
Left alone our balmily mother
Shed with blood nothing other
Whether we are under impure will
Have common shelter but is well
Tents, ropes seem unity and calm
Spaded dibbled digging down
Bodies are here but souls there
Hope of retreating back where
Again, life will have new evolution
Hatred free would be then creation.

18. Why

Why don't con and at last ail
Edification in coping drabble whole
Full page writings but ruin your soul
Soporific somnambulist in all trails
Goblet, ewer, aqua and wine
All you play is minute prodigal
Where to get shower only hail
Why you carouse now it's mine
Hey in politics incorporated religion
Statue of reality but reputation is rare
Uproar with hidden terror for chair
Elation of triumph in prorogation
Some where women are kneaded down
Young fortunes turned into labour
Rapid duplication and handling grubber
Why to throw dust in eyes of your own
Believe in confraternity hate me and mine
Glue must in human no hostility
Appease with love edification for posterity
But a mark arose how and why?

19. My Lazy Chum

What I use is not same
A bit glutton fat and chaffy
Of good nature and bluff too
Always keep giggling, it's good hey
Oh! His charity not dubitable
Ha! His thoughts and firm passion
About Eden and GOD, he is indelible
Mediation about His creation
Stories and tales say the Ramayana whole
How smart he is in oratorio
A couple troupe of one soul
Yes! Moulded in natural tattoo
Mad in his Job intensely he dabble
Is there someone, no care no matter?
If would same why then idle
Alert my chum poesy utter
Give up plodding peep round
Plunge in fair or in fan's fun
Dew is life and death is moan
*Swig the taste as it is RUN RUN**

20. When I Lost It

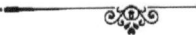

When I lost it in fortissimo
A bit fault, drabble in my motto
Of fair chuckle, tickle in core,
Of eternal coma eke no more
Tale of my heart incur in soul
Get rid of zoo intend to goal
Favour end with romantic knell
Of heaven blossom or foully hell
Why do live if blotch in reputation,
Equal to death, mere cremation
Emotional step why heart relay
The alpha and omega of mine
What's in it salute to challenge
Smile on lips never think of revenge
Fight against it and take it easy.
A day will be there remain her crazy.

21. Day Dreamer

Always think of going to the top
Bright are hopes but dark is pot
Dream of climbing over and over
Only gabble nothing did cover
Dream and dream dawn or eve
Moot at topics remain few
Phantasmal accustomed is so frail
Never move always trail
Have you heard of this fairy tale?
Million, billion he cajoles.
Bus, truck, car or aeroplane
Director actor finally vain
Nothing remain out of dream
Morning begins with having Ace
Evening approaches and ends his race

22. Always Smile

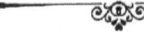

Ever smile ye ever smile
Keep thy annoyance for a while
What's that which made you sad?
To remain in meditation is so bad
What is that makes thee ail
Repeat again if you fail
What had cozened your mind
All that gloom, a smile will bind
No matter if cheated in fair
Why pin heart allow to air
Degradation and giggle have to bear
Where is the strain, smile o dear?
Confliction, contradiction in hut if arise
No need to arouse that's wise
If more drastic keep it aside
By love and talk smile so wide
Of alone and no to babble
Talk with nature no can cavil
With heart and soul, thee grow
Heartily smile in poetic bow
No need to worry o my friend
Smile o dear forever till end

23. I Am Not Blind

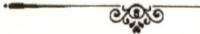

An old and orbed in glasses
Leaned, stilted but the Boss of bosses
Tawny but of good height
Co-walkers left and right
Once upon a time I see
On the stage, hey! Blind ye
An oratorio an echo so sweeter
Juvenescence emerges when lips utter
A rhythmic interlock there prolong
Fingers, device, lips and song
God at rest by giving away
All creative zeal in music-ee-hey!
A bit chats on an autograph please
Recognized voice he ceases.
You know why? No need
In whole crop I am the weed
Master is there me mere gew- gaw
He is owner ripen or raw,
What's there why to mind?
Rejoice if I am not blind.

24. Bachelor Hoot

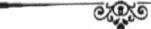

A trip to have a glimpse of nature
Bachelor hoydens and tutor
Of mixed echo jaunty and frisky
Hoyden damsel and jiltee
Slowly puffed four-wheeler
Occupied bachelor, Hoyden in other
Echo accompanied by supervisor
But in way chaotic babble
Dance, hooting, noise so hazel
All the way snout open
Impale me others even
Retreating back was romantic
Jaunty fellow makes dramatic
Abuse accuse to their tutors
Never relies who has the halter
Interrupt a few but mischief prevails.
Let them do will steadily ail
Fault is rare cause is greater
Forego them, mediate jingo creator.

25. Slander Me

Why I had affection and call thee mine
Sympathy of mine borrowed a blotch
Accused of magic with man of thine
Mine refusal of that black act
But with kin traitor and rook
Known to him how I react
Falsehood can even push to nook
Eternal belief enhance faith of mine
Truth and sin what a buzzer
Prove my truthfulness no bloody brine
Increase my purity ever and further
So their false stain
Useless and vain
Mine purity only He knows
But sometime in heart it grows

26. Crazy Tutor

In acidic hall
He used to call
Damsels in preference
Others in absence
With him he keeps a book
Eyes, face fair glances
Throbbing heart and fairy look
May thinking of romance
Fair giggle see so bright
For others wait and wait
In fair Eden he use to ride
You tutor why thee treat
In two parts so apart
Dozy, crazy not so alert
Invalid seed infected crop
What's belle what's dame
Nothing is there in the names
It seems that will breed same

27. True Mother

A country was celebrating in welcome
Of next king which later turned
In tragedy but bright appearance
His mother waited eagerly but burned
When he told her that crown turned into exile
Dad orders and I have to obey but thee
Now I can't stay more for a while
Let your sister enjoin and free
News in charter she fainted down
Pillowed her head remain calm
Hey Mom it is imprecation why to moan
She comes back and awake
Being mom she cursed her fate
That why God bless me with you
It was better if remains in hate
I am eldest of all queens but You
She treats me not so good but will tolerate
Why God has kept me here
I think it will be end of my pain and fate
Heaven; it will be better there

Now I am remorseless what's of mine
Prayers and kindness all in vain
I too like exile which is fine
How can the Cow live without a calf, oh man?
Younger declared, will not tolerate exile
I will fight against the imperial rule
I will teach Dad of women craze in a while
It's cruel...................
You know father's command for a son
Have to obey and shouldn't hate
Have to tolerate what is in one's fate.
Hey! Cadet I know you love me
Mother is in twinge but wouldn't devote
Path is of truth you can't stop me
Do not bring in mind family hate
He requested her mother to let him go
Father is after God you know.
I have no discrimination of younger and elder
She too loves me but what against rebuke
Please do not provoke a confliction further
At last she said, I cannot persuade
You may go let me not moan
Pity! Grassy plush and tree shade
You have to bear leaves and thorn grown

Hey! Prince you firmly believe on reality
There you in forest in pluvial
Here my isolation and apathy
Will pass on or gradually ail
At last she said your advice was right
We should obey imperial rule
Hey! Babe you're firm and true
I would not stop, you can go
Eyes will eagerly, wait for thee
Please impersonate, you and go
She kisses his brow and prays about
Also advised him truth to prove,
Let me kiss Mom your holly feet
Desolation for fourteen when he moves....
Moms have to wait for his arrival
But for his separation she always ails.

28. Their Departure

When they went in palace for departure
In every nook was fatal news
When king hear his heart triggered
And call queens to have their views
He bowed and requests his father
Please allow me to go for exile
Cadet and Hoyden are other
I prevent but they insist for a while
Babe! I wouldn't prevent you from going
Accept day hospitality for sake of father
Tomorrow will be your, you be owing
Babe! Only for me not for other
Wealth is useless to kept your promise
You're my God as you're my Dad
Please crown younger that's wise
He's same as me otherwise it would be bad;
Father on insisting allowed
They begged for exile dress
Their young mom quickly followed
Brother wore his ouphe too kisses

But she doesn't know how to put on
He helps her and folk moan.
He kisses his father and goes on
Other two do same people mourn
At last they ride upon battle cart
Father peeps from top of the palace
For last glance of Gods creative art
Mothers too but have to embrace
They left a moan and city mourn all
In woods at last they disappear
Whatever they had they left there

29. In Dream

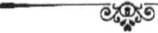

Once in my sleep
In a crowded street
Through bus and vale so deep
Passengers ah! Sheet over sheet
Noise smoke and heat
Oh! Mine breath-breath..........
I stranger, no one to meet
Hate in house teach-teach
Confusion in mind
Where I going be
All alone nature around
When they dropped me
I smile because I am away
From dirty noise of island
In nature hey...
Beauty if which perfectly grand
The wild come said why are alone
Then in a minute a bus came,
Me, the wild and a driver
Move along river-river

The wild dropped me alone,
Try to break this trap
But how to come down
Only reflects of stab and stab
A cool pool, why? Avoid eddy?
Will steal or be ready
Mine face moist was with dew
I refused sword he drew
Took me away and beat
What cool only heat and heat
To save life, I agreed
And the boss showed me
Will this likely breed
In this tomb your room lee
Condition of tomb unbearable
Women, gal, children and other
Was all unbearable?
From nook and corner they were gathered
How to fly away
Who'll take us away?
Hands of children were cutlass
They teach them begging
Women were used to romance
Refusal results in hanging

I saw, few of them bloody
Orbs tear unable to endure
By isolation I cure
Once in haste, I refuse to murder
Smother him was an order
To divert them away
I finally obey
Once I committed a mistake
In woods they give me a push
Hedges of thorns and bushes
Terror of dagger so I make haste
Give me water was my last wish
They trained me as world don
Spurring of weapon
Decoct head in the crown
Once I started go on and on
That day was mine I prefer to escape
Jumped down from fifth stage
Made my habitat in dense forest
Where is the direction east or west?
There I saw a house but no men
It was haven of scorpion and snake
Following me were secretary and men
From window a narrow escape

Men were nowhere but she followed me
Bare footed in the forest
My trick works and I hide from she
At the top of the hill I take a rest
As it dawned I hear some voices
All these brutal were in my search
I run down through precipices
But she finished her work
While running I stumbled
Then I know her treating
She triggered a gun but trembled
I snatch the pistol and break it
She had a knife but threw
Embraced me saying few
Oh! The whole sight changes
Two enemies were now friends
Then eyes in eyes
Hand in hand and all alone
She assured me by kissing
Reply of mine, a proper rejoicing
She hangs like a garland
With arms around
Tears in eyes and face russet red
Roses in lips and clouds in hair

With enemy how she dare
I felt bells were ringing in ear
Her look revelled how she bear
Declared that she must have escaped
But had not got a chance to flee
That's why here with thee
How extremely she memorize her family
Fortune treated her badly
Her narration kept me tearing
Let us run away from that suffering
Be my peg and me be your garland
Suddenly awakened oh! Pillow in hand
In my heart she shall remain
And will keep hunting for same
I meet her occasionally in my sleep
And she is eternal in my dream.

30. Youth and Nation

Come together oh you youth
Dwelling in dark turn to truth
Do you have cardiac emotions?
Let's join hands to uplift the nation
Bodies are there and would not be
It will decay and soul will flee
Sons and daughters of the mother
Forget our melee and come together
Let's join hands
And established a band
To improve the nation
Our salutary creation
Where humanity is why is terrorism
How can we get rid of nihilism?
Have to expose incognito
There is difference in face and heart
Have to remove from the nation's path
Troubles are more and need endurance
Have to evacuate is trial of tolerance
Here in society evils prevail

From which an innocent ail
Have to remove as possible
Use it if need is forcible
What made you sleepless? The corruption!
That had trekked the progress of my nation
Poor father how can you afford
Money plays when future accord
If you think top
But I am the root
But I am the root
Invalid seed infected crop
Oh! My mother, oh! You dear
Why this disgrace and tears
How much and to what extent will thee bear
This body and every drop of blood is thine
This breadth is yours what is mine
She bestows everything without any discrimination
Why then we can't enjoy as nation
Confliction among us is mere ravine
Are there words to praise the glory of thine?
No but Youth will stake for sake of thine

31. In the Lake

In a happy dell charming around
Covered green with forest wide
When in boat we found
Core of earth water aside
In the lap of the heaven
Rippling mute in golden shine
Rejoice under aquatics too
Carps, turtle and shadow of mine
A trail of life if drowned
O! Wonder what's there underneath?
Here the life is dwelling around
How the harmony flourishes beneath
In her lap a life how life mound
Agonies dispelled remain free
From human, guns and knives
Let's enjoy if here are we
It was more beautiful when a fair bid
Bye, thanks I too add
How gladly human rejoice
Who has good luck?
Me the human or bird the duck

32. The Grazier and the Nymph

Comical was he pleasantly passing smile
Grasping twine and sickle in nape
Playing flute and travels mile
Wearing turban a jaunty shape
How friendly he followed cattle
Herd of sheep, cows, oxen and calf
Drove them and smiles a little
Neither he is tall nor is he dwarf
Echinate is way and remote is hamlet
Pastures are green around the hamlet
And in meadow once he had a sudden nap
Dream was sweet with the fair nymph
She watched cattle and he lays in her lap
He was ecstatic with his triumph
He wake up and what he found
A fragrance speared all around
Dangling flowers, pleasant air
Humblebees with buds near
In her lap, in spite of ground
Her beauty moulded in skill

Sweet quizzical for a while
Apple round, russet face
And her mad sight kills
An innocent grazier of human race
She uttered an affable tune
Fingers on flute then move
Eternal echo in sky so flew
Nature predicts, fortunate few
Took oath for whole life
Swear as husband and wife
Their day passed in full rejoice
Isolation of nights was agonizing
In musical tune and affable voice
How smoothly was their life running?
While sitting at the edge of stream
He was musing in dream
Nature played and tides swept
With waves he rolled to heaven
He was mortal but she was soul
In isolation she was left
She still seeks him in meadows.
How many times her songs are heard
The tune of loneliness singing lonely
Now and forever she is left only

33. You Move They Pull

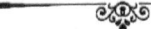

Democratic, social and secular my nation
Where are my duties and where are rights?
In this salutary creation
No space for violence, no to fight
You want to be leader but who'll support
Do you know? It's a selfish zoo
Crazy, mad, called people too
Wastage of time what it wrought?
Mouths will be there to urge you mere
The result in the way you will see
Thorns, bushes and you will tear
Will haul you and folk will flee
You would not turn back till bleed
Now see back no one will be there
Only few you ever need
No matter if lonely, passion should be your
Encouragement if you have goal is than your
Pure is always pure, whether in impure
Never give up until you achieve
That you dream and idea you view

34. His Birth

Dark was night and lights went off
Loneliness around in cool breeze
He was born in her green lap
In the starlit who plunged him.
Sweet was his lilt in her lap
Under, blue roof and on green floor
I saw him lying over
Cursing creator in his blubber
Stained in blood in grassy cover
Fortunately in her perpetual lap
Caste, creed no matter no bar
We make division, but she never like
What religion, mere we follow all.
How easily she tolerates
Selfless love no space to hate
Will he know his mother and father?
What would be his future further?
Will he play with sisters and brothers?
Who know how he descended

35. Why Beat Against the Wall

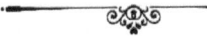

Have you ever faced bleeding?
When you try head against the wall
It is agonising and everlasting
Hundred times but fail
Nothing results in it all
Same is the case when
You dream of climbing
A hill in which no men
Had ever conquered
Think what you can or you cannot
To shoot stars from the sky
Without wings you want to fly
Never handle which you can't nab
You handsome Mac or beautiful Mab
Practical minds have no barriers of wall
But reflect to make the way
That will dismantle it all.
And there will be goal in the way

36. You Were

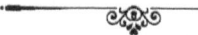

Once and forever you were
Universal eternal now you are
Handsome in youth, wise you old.
Leave behind glitter and turned to gold
As gradually you grow old
Truth and justice you try to mould
Illuminate lamp where stagnation holds
Thy prayers nigh you to God
Wise, infallible, true and nimble
Few complexities remain inextricable
At last thee breathe thine last
But after death you send the lass
Akin to Goddess genius she was
Where thee left from there she starts
Probably she will go ahead flawless
And will fulfil the dream thine was

37. Revenue Chain

Benediction of chain do you know
Let me pay a reverent bow
Being member let me tell
Ferrous chain shots tied well
Five less than three score
And can be added if need is more
Mob presents themselves like silly coot
Entrapped easily in my coop
When this chain if mine
Tied neck if thine
You would seek shelter in chain's coping
I will pull it hard until crying
Finally you will obey man
Then I will salute to my chain
Hitherto I haven't told you something
Area increases by a single jerk
That's the principle how it works
And is overload of revenue mete
Source of earning and heart beat
Honest use can put end of melee

Trick in it dignity will flee
I smack it and work is my process
No greed no metempsychosis

38. True Answer

I have an idle brain
It is futile what can I drew
Stressing upon it is in vain
But answer must true
No need to be glutton
If tasteless you have eaten
Would it promote you?
No not at all
Asked would you flung a wall
False! That you can do.
But in a way you come across
Than would beat against the wall
If blotched answer true
Why greed of a crown
Meaning of what is not known
Will cheat mob less
Then you yourself
Being silver you coat the gold
Why do so, why you mould
Glitter for a while

Forever old
Pledge for purity of soul
So need is true answer

39. Life

Once we are born will never come again
Endure it friendly either precise or fault
Body is your and you are human
Believe ,will never come again
For me it has five marvellous ages
Gradually descend not evergreen.
What is ours? It's spontaneous
Mystery of soul it has been
Up to one score it is careless
You be the babe gradually grows
Ridiculous, mischievous demand new dress
On birth date or the festival you know
It's free of discrepancy
Whatever exists no matter for you?
Ha! Ha happiness and agony
Mom and Dad it's for you
A decade breeds same for all
After some decked other tumbling
Stocks, spades, mud besides all
Peeps in the world of care and love

Starts emerging the sign and symptoms
Career hunt, for some here glows
Next is the age of lover
Dreams struck every mind and heart
Mere remain childish no never
Think around you and seem alert
Some espoused and others in fair
With ecstatic number or eclogue
In the shade of curls o! My dear
Eyes are goblets and curls are shade
It is juvenescence where all wade
Now you will be called as Mom and Dad
These two take almost two score
And third begin of bullock
Same they do or it's more
Abdomen wants tread every track
Yoked pair cooped for earning
To produce more for offspring
Have to plough whether it's hard
Desires there touched infinity
Not mere cup but claim whole
Not for them but think of posterity
If hope is there can stake their soul
This hard work make human impotent

Consign to sixty and precede more
Everything feeble and impatient
Eve of third and coping near four
You are sensible, you are wise
Advice, order, command and anger
Same were ancestors than you realise
Earlier you think they may hinder
So it's of terrier and vexation
Cause of noise and perch in hand
To every melee you think of melioration
You have skill so thine is the wand
You never bear that entire prodigal
Oh! Scooped me you the testy
Hey why ask about my tonsil
Please consign not so frisky
Last and final is above four score
So here starts reverse counting
Mutter from snout and crooked more
Brat, urchin laugh at hiccoughing
Twisted like an owl sunken eye
Source of saliva, house for flies
Squalid crouched appear really owl
Tickled if can only growl
Sight in dark or light has same range
Waiting to knell and no care
Now think of sins and no revenge

Give up me mine and turn to mediation
Advice people of sins and faults
Body is useless after spirit separation
What I have harvested ,don't be a part.
Earlier I thought it was everything
What I use it was mine
But now I am realising
Whatever you give that is thine
Embarrassment, agonies show patience
These are your friends keep in tolerance
Be neutral if you can't do better
Ephemera has only one day
Sunrise with its birth and set it dies
Enjoy this life in this way
Unpredictable quiz or water bubble
Top and bottom of which is not known
Forecast of which is mere to dabble
Enjoy jubilantly, it finally groan
Struggle, firmness and spiritual fight
Havoc with it violence can play
Duties are if yours you have rights
Its mere play and we are troupes
Show concludes with falling curtain
Epilogue of which is fixed and certain

40. Prince and Princess

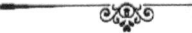

They were two kids in tale
The king and other in defence
Only love nurture no annoyance
But later this love stale
Emperor had an astute nymph
Other a had a son but not alert
Excess care makes him strut
The daughter was parents triumph
She was moulded in perfect tips
The God has used all his skill
In Eden Goddess she will
Sculptured eyes and moulded lips
How calmly she respects her elders.
Voice so sweet like the cuckoo,
Roses are less fragrant in odour
She talks in ease with little murmur.
Both had same schooling
And enjoy same class
She was talented and devoted to her heart.
But her cousin was nurtured apart.

The news spread all around
The cousin found losing his ground.
What he has never thought
Then there it was wrought.
Root was one and one was blood
Enjoy the sun and have the same clouds.
World of material become hostile
Reconciliation was futile
Emperor wanted his daughter to be crowned
Day approached and hostility breeds
During her bath she was pushed into sea
In Palace they pretend of mishap
They assumed she has been died
Along the sea was travelling man
He had spade rope in his hand
Gather wood into a bale
He found life in her
When it seemed that she was breathing
Open eyes and start some eating
She enquired that why she ail
He uttered the whole tale
At first sight she fell in love
Feelings for him were unexpressed
Rare to separate and move

Of his honesty she was impressed
The traveller saw her once in woods
Went to palace and narrate the truth
The mourn of fort turned into happiness
She is alive was really a mystery
Everyone murmur it may be history
One-month cheer back to sadness
She now hated the life in palace
Was accustomed of living in eternity
Huts, greenery and wild race
Missed all, retreated indirectly
Rabid cousin leer at her
Truth of her death was still hidden
Folk there ooze in tears
But her cousins still have leers.
Crocodile tears heart forbidden
She told her father about the lad
Who rescued me is that man
An epitome should get reward
Emperor offered but in vain
He firmly refused to take
He furiously left the palace
She and her friends went to see it.
Her eyes had requests and pleas.

They overheard the lyric of love
All of them burst into tears.
He sings and the tone is clear.
Let's hear...... Let us hear
I just wished to have your glimpse
And was thirsty of your appearance
Want thee oh my nymph
I can't wait, its end of my tolerance.
Everything in you I want to owe
Just you surrender O! My love
I love thee but can't utter.
You my love life would be better
Something that you too may
That's what I want to say
She too had something to say.
You are my lot I have to owe.
Together the life we can row
The melody really touched her heart
She returned back and said
I shall marry that wild lad
Either will die so be alert
On the other hand,
Enemies accumulate a huge band.
Oh! Loon why you relume

The spark again resumes.
Later was covetous for the crown
Why daughter, son, my own.
Her beloved was entangled in trick
He has to be hanged the crime was false
Proven guilty without fault
She knows their cunningness and discovered
But yet she had not exposed
The trick that they had played
What's thy choice prior to death?
I want the glimpse of my breath
Permission was granted and kept alone
When he saw her was unable to mumble
Forget the sentence and recall the days
Together they spent all the way
She was going to lost her own
Fight in the family for the crown
She had found the loon's trick
To her father she exposed it
He has not thought of this mystery
How the brother can be hostile
Against the emperor, turn the whole legion.
Family was forced to leave that region
However her love was recruited in legion

Now the family has life of exile
Luxuries of palace were no more
Possibilities of life they have to explore
Other hand brother has crowned his son
They had kingdom and they had fun
What had happened known to none
In the solitude both has to run
Either side heart has to burn
Smoke of which went into sky
In memories they use to fly
Emperor had ordered dead or alive
He has intention to remove the thorn
That later can hurdle his way
The platoon seek them all the way
The lad found but never revealed
No hostile oh! My dear
They are alive chance is rare
I need the leave for a week
In spite of home he went there
Charming calm meek and meek
Soothing air every where
No pains no agonies
That past had poured on them
Oh! Mine prince how I miss

This isolation quenches my breath
He in response offered a kiss
It took years them to meet
For a week they miss the world
He retreats back all alone
Her isolation was now tears and cries
He used to leave with play and lies
One day the falsehood has to sway
Will not breed in the same way
Once they were caught in embrace.
Both exult in willow's shade.
Legion at last has chased.
He surrenders and lets her flee.
Was sentenced and put behind bars.
Everything is fair in love and war.
Both have given up the trust of life.
Have to reap raw no hope of ripeness.
Her heart triggered but gave up grievance.
She has decided to exploit this sentence.
She impersonate herself as soldier
She entered the palace without any fear
Day of victory was celebrated there
She had intoxicated the ewer.
Mere drinks make them slumber.

Strategy works and slaves were free
Morn dawn and troops chase
Both running the love race
Again they lost in the romantic world.
Eyes in eyes hand in hands
Oh! See that drastic enemy band.
It is the end of love of this mine
Response keen forever was thine.
Storms out the rain of tears
Movement later the world will disappear.
See the horizon in the sky.
There in the love will fly.
Wow! His Hero Chum
Come with troops of his own
Where from he descended was not known.
Playing bugles with rhythmic drums
Battle finally he had won
Defeats hostile wow! Power
That had not been seen ever
Family assembled altogether
Wild got the crown as prince
My choice sighed princess
Wow! Price princess kingdom
Wow prince princess kingdom

41. Death of Pigeon

It pays debt of nature
Cause of death was not known
On the grassy ground
Its body was found.
Shrivelled, crouched wet in dew,
May it died of climate change
May be temperature in acute range
But mob had different view
There in eyes I found the clue
May in hope of returning
From nest left an offspring
Which flew away but do not returned
Chirp was caught by the fair damsel.
She for the half an hour
Kept chirp and talk for a while
Probably she loved birds
But it resisted imprisonment
So she gave it away.
Her kind heart let it free
Not known where it flee

May it be the cause?

And responsible may she was

But not its nature

Died too was still in wait

Of its offspring

Here its eyes revealed.

42. In Your Absence

Intolerable is thine absence
Alone my heart squeeze
Oh it stopped why it froze.
Eyelids dry with no furtherance.
No impulse and cease the breath
Winking eyes in complete doze
Lure there in your face
The shadow of which I use to trace
Gleaming bud of this world
Like an Empress in your world
Same for me as usual too
You fair Lad of this zoo
And then comes your eclogue
Echo of sweetness tangle around
Fly in air spread on ground
What was there in thine song?
Affection was there make me wrong
Hey! You are not alone
You would be never alone
I am with you

And I would be with you forever
Soul of mine is thine
Suddenly I wake and was truly alone
Only your voice tangle in ear
Whether at distance or near
Eternal, you will be everywhere.
I think I'm ephemeral and alone
Thine imagination and you say.
Hey................................
You are not alone
You would never be alone
I am with you
This soul of mine is thine
I am yours and you are mine
And I will forever be thine

43. Picture

Think of you in Imagination
From where is descended this creation
How paper bear you so cute
Calm, cool, real and mute
In your picture
Lips, round, roral dialogue.
Seem singing an eclogue
Really sweet, tangle in air
Silent words in my ear
Compare thee no one there
Akin nightingale
In your picture
Round, red, russet face
That is how the God has traced
Probably by mistake
Skilled incarnation with no haste
In your picture
Do your Eyes have glittering stars?
That shoots an innocent in a war
Revealed how cruel you are

Trapped him in thine curls
How dark are these whorls?
Entrapped him forever as slave
That is why he fell in love
In your picture
You are of stately height
Thine treading is absolutely light
In thine corset
In your picture
Unaware probably is the creator
He has not noticed a new creature
Else He would have fallen in love
Before that he will see
I will hide thee
In my heart
So apart
Maculation you would not owe
In your picture

44. Why You Play

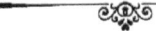

Mine heart is yours why ye break.
Of that act shall always shake
You did so if I was a doll.
I was fragile why you roll
Once you have respected my dignity.
Now you called it blotched and dirty
Do you know?
The cruelty you owe.
Now where will you keep this act of thine?
It will be a curse at the heart of thine.
Break the promise of walking together.
Pains of life and sorrows rather.
Absolute it was do you know
Nothing in return I need, you owe
You play so let you glow
I am the lonely there in to row

45. I and Thee

Desire is to be with thee.
There you embrace me.
Let us both boom in Eden
Restricted and love forbidden
Hate on earth provoke them to stab
Chance they missed here they grab
Auscultation of my own
Again there I found
Felt no difference in beat
Are reliable and can't cheat.
You are always same
In thee I haven't seen any change
But a dream, false it seems.
That is there what I mean

46. Cob Web

Of thine eyes divine strike in
Core of my heart babe you win
Gleam brightly your future hey
Shrine is little but I always pray
Idol of mine your priest caged in
Your smile keeps me within
Come to me why you sway
Embracing together is another way
Lips within lips bosoms with chest
Let's have an auscultation test
Let's together quench our thirst
Never imagine of separating now
Let, s twist and roll tonight
Never want to leave cobweb

47. Tears

When ooze out it is rare
But my heart bleeds into tears
Both of us had common shelter
Locked voices how to utter
Veiled orbs rare to peep
So my heart tears deep
How stride far when you were near
You make me alone you make me tear
Sweet dreams together are now a nightmare.
Why you play with my heart
Babe you treat it as a toy but it is part.
How you turned off with no care
You presented and I have to bear
And now, my isolation with me
Once you were but you flee
I have to go with that nightmare
With my new care "The Tears"

48. Just You

What's that you have own
Natural it has been grown
I can't exist without thee
How firm is my belief in thee?
Wow! His creative devotion
All stuff of beauty he has spend
Where form He bring that notion?
From beginning to the end
As you glow sun can't be
Hundred times more you glee
How inspirational are the buds
As it dawn it grow till evening it fades
In this short duration wind can sheds
But everlasting will go ahead
How shiny is Dew in dawn
Sprinkled over grass like diamonds
Hours sun shine it's no more
Thine gleaming shall ever alike
Even hot and cold changes its course
Its natural routine of climate

No alteration in thee shall arouse
You will be same up to universal date
Soothing air fragrance around
Of waving rivers tides to lull
There I and you hand in hand
Engaged in talking along river's fluxion
Tracing thine footprints over the sand
Mediate about the marvellous creation
Romantic couple in willow's shade
In thine arms I shall ride
There will be no one at least
Thou be idol and I be the priest
Idolatries thee sprinkling divine
Idolize thee just facing east
There I will be yours and you'll be mine
Promising thee of not letting down
You reply "that is wise "
Here I am your own
With thine sorrows and with thy pains
Nothing shall harm hot or rain
Always be mine and go ahead
You breathe and it gives me life
Make me glee is thine smile
Never go away whether hell or heaven

Spirits shall travel and have a tryst
In the world of sylphs you will be one
And your priest along my princess
Epitome of beauty compares none
Be my candle as I am your moth
Will gyrate around thine flame
As on earth keep the same

49. Cute and Shiny

Why moon faded in dark night
You glitter more and are bright.
Thine repose and mine surrender
Words of affection when you render
New life there your presence brought
Sensation of yours triggered my heart
Why so cute why so calm
The night is thine and yours is the lot
Souls united and breathing balm
How closely you embrace me
Shadows of thine foretop make it darker
My heart and bosoms of thine
Your auscultation same as mine
Moon said, forgive I have to go
Let me see you tomorrow
I Plea to stay, but thee
With kiss bade goodbye
In moon light how you flee
Leaving me alone

50. Cheater

Babe you get rid of me
Here you escape and you are free.
I saw in club your fans too
Swigging in romance hey you
How innocently you break my heart
Showed your cruelty but I am alert
You can't cheat me now
How false is thine love?
In my dreams there you go
Was it merely the puppet's show?
But here I am waiting still
To the sunrise above the hill

51. I Am Waiting

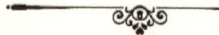

Eyes are tired of prolonged waiting
What could be the reason, you are late
I was worried of that wait
You love me true but can't express
Utter a word it will be your kindness
Relations within heart are unbreakable
You are little away
A step more, you will achieve hey
Want to hear you so I am waiting
Summer it is and buds are smiling
Don't wait for autumn everything will wither
Nor will I. You will be neither.

52. You Cruel

In your love I drink the divine
Not your infuriate life is mine
You poisoned it whatever it be
Arms pushed and you veiled of me
Then my eyes and heart tear.
Either of them no matter for you
Where thee an exhibition known
Fair but callousness broke down
Now summer lacks blooming flowers
Not in fate formerly over
Cape of agonises had given love the crown
How to hold it being broken down
I have brightness forever to owe
You pushed me cruelly into shadows

53. It Is Mine

Arrows of thine eyes are nothing to my heart
Once you broke, can't be your part
In her lobby she knocked me down
Now how can you say I am your own?
Are you habitual of swearing and cheating?
Cape once tore no need of weaving
Mirror is transparent until it is broken
How carefully you glue the spots are there.
Separation in fate, it's my own
If ruined, no reason to moan.
She is one but hundreds are there.
Seek your love may be hidden somewhere
Anywhere else will be thine fate
Go on steadily make no haste

54. Your Magic

I can't leave you oh my love
You are mine everything how can a I go
You drive me by your magic
Is it fair or it is tragic
Can leave easily , can't broke heart
In my life laurels you brought
I haven't forgotten my promise
Of being together as one
No narration to praise you creature
Sun get ashamed in this nature
Divine of thine eyes, caroused me
It provoked me to hold thee
Sometimes I think I will lose
No way will I bear the bruise.

55. My Own

Fascinated and caroused of thine trace
Soporific eyes it's your face
Why are you away o my own
Curled upright and breathing balm
Garden well but rose petal one
To have the glimpse I travel a mile
I will keep thee in my eyes
There it will have real fame
I will call them with your name
Near to my heart or away from me
O my goddess I will worship thee
As you are my own
The reason unknown
Whatsoever only you are my own

56. For You

Why in the world creature are loving
Once happiness into hundreds tearing
Several friends and their sensibility
Some are dear other breed hostility
Low and high contradiction have spoiled several lives
Love is sold and promises are for lies.
In this fair world, whom will you bow?
Your salute is vacant that you owe
Auscultation of yours to whom will you say
Everyone is deaf useless hey
Entangle in it why are you?
These are lyrics for you.

57. Memories

Why the memories shock me everyday
Why they call me everyday
It's only our affection
Growing day by day
They come near give me smile
And I feel happy for a while
When they shock me again
Give me a sensation of pain
How lucky to meet with you.
Can I spend more with you?
Can I forget I spent with you?
When I will far away from you
The memories will shock me again and again
Thanks my God he is great
Who met us but too late
Memories of our childhood will not come again
And memories will shock me again and again
Why are going away from me
Why is it so please tell me?
My heart will break with pain

And the memories will shock me again and again
When I am far away from you
My wet eyes will find you
And I will cry with great pain
And your memories will shock me again and again

58. A True Friend

A true friend is one
Who is better other than
Helping you in trouble
And does not put in hurdle
Encourage you to work hard
So that you can achieve its reward
Does not lead you on the wrong path
Advices you, to believe in God
Who shares joy and sorrow with you
That's true friend.

www.ingramcontent.com/pod-product-compliance
Lightning Source LLC
La Vergne TN
LVHW091530070526
838199LV00001B/11
* 9 7 8 9 3 5 8 1 9 8 8 3 6 *